Bush Terminal International Exhibit Building And Buyers Club

Bush Terminal Company

In the interest of creating a more extensive selection of rare historical book reprints, we have chosen to reproduce this title even though it may possibly have occasional imperfections such as missing and blurred pages, missing text, poor pictures, markings, dark backgrounds and other reproduction issues beyond our control. Because this work is culturally important, we have made it available as a part of our commitment to protecting, preserving and promoting the world's literature. Thank you for your understanding.

Bush Terminal International Exhibit Building & Buyers' Club

The Building devotes three floors to a Buyers' Club with unusual conveniences for its members. The Club in connection with the exhibition rooms and private offices, makes the building the Buying Centre of the world, a vast centralized market place under one roof where complete sample lines of goods can be examined without loss of time. The Bush Terminal Company invites your inspection of the Building

Copyright 1917
by
Bush Terminal Company
New York

To Manufacturers and Merchants

WE DO not aim to rent this building, and then leave it to work out its own success. We purpose making it such a success that you cannot do without it. We know that you will not be a permanent tenant, unless we save you money and increase your sales. We are not lightly spending two million dollars, and a million more for a Service Building and facilities to supplement it. Some Exhibition Buildings have failed because they have been real estate propositions—attempts to fill an unproductive building. This building will succeed, because its location was selected and the structure equipped for its purpose, and it has underlying it the Bush Terminal plant with all its service. We are creating a permanent institution, and plan to spend hundreds of thousands of dollars to attract and keep customers for you. If we do not do this, *you* will make a trifling loss and terminate your lease, but we will make a large loss, and endanger the entire prestige of our success. Who takes the risk? Can we afford to see you lose?

Irving T. Bush

International Exhibit Building
of the
Bush Terminal Company
130-2 West Forty-second Street
New York City

Bush Terminal
International Exhibit Building New York

Its Significance to Manufacturer and Buyer

THE opening of the Bush Terminal International Exhibit Building is an event of tremendous importance to American manufacturers and to buyers the world over. It is commercially unique; without a precedent. Its possibilities and objects are many; its aim high; its success assured. By bringing producer into direct contact with buyer, under the most favorable circumstances and conditions, it forms absolutely the last word in sales efficiency

Located in Times Square, New York, in the very center of the World's marketplace, the Exhibit Building is designed to present a complete sample display of the world's goods.

Because New York is the trade center, hundreds of thousands of buyers, from everywhere, buying everything, visit the city from one to six times a year. New York, more than ever before, is the vital place for the manufacturer to show his products. And further, the Bush Terminal International Exhibit Building is pre-eminently the place for him to display them, for the building offers the

This corridor gives one the feeling of England one hundred years ago

out-of-town buyer attractive and advantageous opportunities not to be found elsewhere.

The buyer finds, no matter what goods he seeks to purchase, a complete line of samples, perfectly displayed. He has, within the building, the comforts of a well-appointed club, the advice of domestic and foreign sales experts, stenographic and clerical help, telephone, telegraphic and cable communication with the whole world, daily bulletins, giving price quotations, changes and important news of his business, all current periodicals, a general library and a rare collection of reference books; every chance for transacting his firm's business quietly, in one place, with dispatch and efficiency. Such possibilities were never before within his reach. He is bound to transact New York business in the building, for he can save twenty-five per cent. of effort and accomplish twice as much by so doing. Incidentally, the building, because of its location in the center of the business, shopping, hotel

One of the many quiet corners

and amusement district, its nearness to all railway terminals and direct connection with steamship lines, makes another strong appeal to him.

Taken together, these factors, aids to manufacturer and buyer—as essential to each other as capital and labor—form the strongest of sales inducers and trade builders. As a soap manufacturer said to a musical instrument buyer, when the project had been outlined to them: "Why a man doesn't need eyes to 'see' this proposition," and the business interests of these men give idea of the industries represented.

The Foyer elevators give an unsurpassed service to the showrooms

A section of the Club which shows how the Gothic feeling
has been carried out

The Building

The Building proper is the crystallization of a dream of many years; it represents an investment of $2,000,000. In no sense is it a hurried, slighted undertaking. On the contrary, every feature has been thoroughly and thoughtfully considered, experts consulted and no pains spared to make it efficient in all details. It is in keeping with the entire Bush organization; the same high standards here appear that have made the Terminal what it is today.

The building itself is thirty stories high, of modernized Gothic architecture—decidedly the most imposing structure in the neighborhood. Design, construction and finish immediately stamp it. The Bush Terminal International Exhibit Building is one of the newest and most interesting sights of New York, and will be open evenings.

Decoration and Arrangement

The interior decoration of the three lower floors, the portion given over to the Buyers' Club, is Old English, giving one the feeling of having entered a hundred-year-old tavern. Comfort is king, with every modern convenience in attendance. The rich, dark red tiles, fine old panelling and appropriate coverings, thick, soft rugs, massive tables with shaded lights, current magazines and writing materials, and tempting chairs, all contribute toward hominess and desirability.

At the left of the Forty-second Street entrance is the information bureau, and opposite a magazine and cigar counter with a theatre ticket office. Beyond is a large foyer or vestibule, with stairs at the left and four elevators at the right. Passing through a corridor, on either side of which are retiring rooms for ladies and gentlemen, a lounge is entered. On the left are stenographers and writing desks, telephone booths, telegraph and cable connections and a news and financial ticker. At the extreme rear, fronting on Forty-first Street, are the Bush Terminal offices for building and club business and a street door.

Special Features

The front portion of the second floor is given over to another lounge, an open well in the center giving glimpse of the lower floor. Back of this is a center lounge and reading room, with coat room and an unrivalled buffet service. The reading room occupies the entire Forty-first Street end of the second, or mezzanine, floor; and no expense has been spared to have this room meet with the demands and requirements asked. The collection of data for reference use is complete; theories, facts and figures of every industry, kept up-to-date by articles published in trade journals and new books, are accessible; trained librarians, besides the foreign and domestic sales experts, together with standard works on buying and selling merchandise, complete a room such as any and every manufacturer can use to individual advantage.

A corner which carries one back to Early English taverns

A corner in the Art Salon where paintings may be hung

On the third floor are finely-appointed conference rooms, and offices for exhibitors who wish special quarters in addition to their display space. Here also is an auditorium where lectures and concerts may be given, or where exhibitors can, with motion pictures, illustrate their plants and manufacturing process. Fashion parades can be held in the auditorium, the long concourse, with perfect lighting, presenting ideal conditions for displaying gowns.

Throughout these floors, as well as the sections of the basement occupied by the Club, the decoration and furnishings are of the same Old English tone. Portions of the basement not occupied by the Club or building equipment may be used by manufacturers who desire to exhibit machinery. To all exhibits of a mechanical nature, or otherwise, where power is needed to give a working demonstration, power is supplied.

Exhibits

Manufacturers' exhibits completely occupy the twenty-seven upper floors. An efficient ventilating system, complete fireproof building construction, and a thorough system of policing insure all exhibitors against loss. The most modern of lighting systems, that which simulates daylight with eye-strain danger scientifically removed, has been installed; such system, for many kinds of merchandise, is necessary to perfect exhibition. This feature should especially appeal to many manufacturers whose goods are often shown at disadvantage.

It is a simple matter to make sales when goods are displayed as
in the Children's Department

The essential spaciousness is indicated on the
Rug and Drapery floors

Musical Instruments of every description may be shown to the best advantage

Every facility for proper display will be found in the Electrical Goods section

The display facilities in the Men's Furnishings section rival the finest haberdashery shops

All kinds of Goods for Travelers may be shown in this salesroom

A more effective use of case and cabinet arrangement could not be obtained than in the Women's Department

The exhibits on these floors will be explained and cared for by trained salesmen, supplied by the building or exhibitor. The entire floor space, for exhibits, has been divided into units ten feet square. An exhibitor may utilize a single unit. If he desires, this space may be doubled, and in cases of larger exhibits, even more is available. Each floor, if not occupied by a single industry, will be taken up by exhibitors whose products are in some way related.

The Buyers' Club

Membership in the Buyers' Club is free. The only requirement is that a reputable firm authorize one or more buyers of its organization for membership. If their standing entitles them to membership they are enrolled. New members are proposed, and sponsored for in the usual fashion. All the exclusiveness of a large metropoli-

Dark wall panelling and appropriate draperies all combine
to give rich effects

tan club, and that mysterious element called "atmosphere" which makes so for desirability and standing of members, is evident in every part. Already there is a large membership and the roll is growing daily.

With the rapid entry of women into commercial activities, more and more consideration is granted them. In the Buyers' Club adequate provisions have been made for the welcoming of women members.

Exhibitors also enjoy the freedom and use of the club rooms, and reservation for the use of the auditorium,

Comfort is king, with every modern convenience in attendance

motion picture machines, or for the use of the offices or any other convenience—may be made as is done in hotels. The advantages afforded manufacturers by the trade experts and reference literature, in their relation to selling campaigns, are not to be underestimated.

All club business, building upkeep and membership qualification details, are handled right in the building by the Bush Terminal officials. Besides the bulletins, a live and helpful house organ is published, a supplement to the Bush Magazine.

The Merchandise Represented

Among the lines to be represented in the building by exhibits are:

Books, Pictures, Rugs and other Floor Coverings, Draperies, Tapestries, Men's Furnishings, Hats and Haberdashery, Canes and Umbrellas, Shoes and Over-Shoes, White Goods and Women's Wear, Children's Wear and Toys, Household Furnishings, Furniture, Napery and Tableware, Kitchen Equipment, Groceries, Goods for Travelers, Sporting Accessories, Musical Instruments, Electrical Appliances, Laundry Fittings, Small Machinery, and the list is being lengthened daily.

Foreign Extensions

Seeking to internationalize the Bush idea of selling service as exemplified in this new building we have plans under operation for a similar building in London and another in Petrograd. Through our special European representatives the field is now being carefully surveyed, and as soon as feasible our plan will be projected into foreign countries, offering added opportunities to American manufacturers.

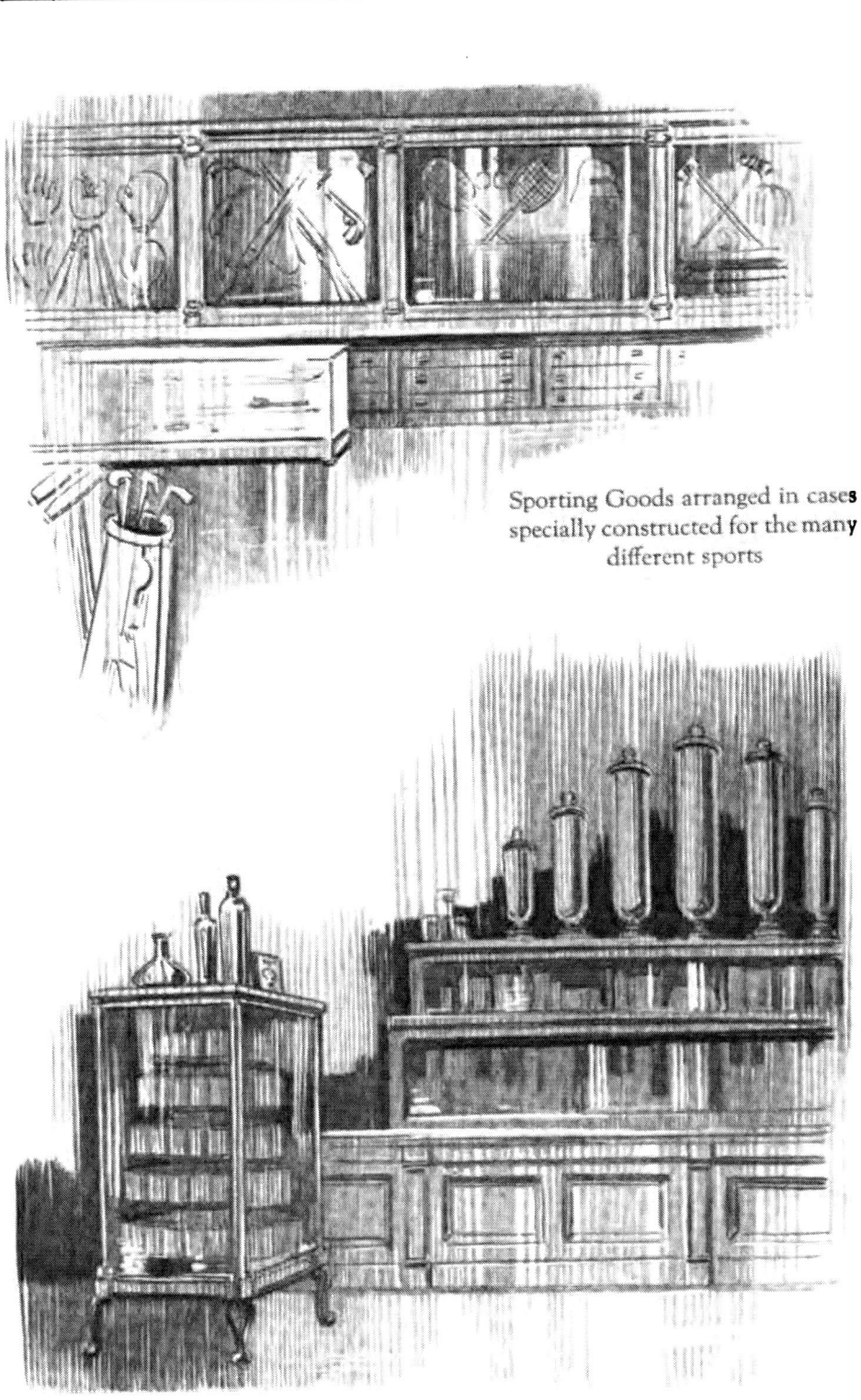

Sporting Goods arranged in cases specially constructed for the many different sports

No wholesale or retail Grocery has a more effective display room

Shipping and Forwarding Service

Economical, effective display and sale of goods are but two arms to the Service offered to exhibitors. The third is expert shipping and forwarding through the facilities of our Service Building, which is the connecting link in the movement of goods from the exhibitor's plant to his customers in Eastern or Export markets.

Through the medium of the Exhibit of Samples and the Salesman-in-charge at the Exhibition Building, goods are sold to buyers who congregate there from both nearby and distant fields. One order taken may have as its destination a seaboard town in the Southern States, another

Probably nowhere else can Kitchen Equipment be shown to better advantage

In the basement facilities are provided to show Small Machinery in operation

may be ordered shipped to a city in the interior of New England, another to South America, another to Russia, and so on.

Instead of making individual shipments, with the obvious trouble, expense and delays, you as manufacturer need only put a carload or any part thereof on track at your factory consigned to Bush Terminal, New York, and forget it. Since Bush Terminal is an official destination point recognized by all railroad and steamship lines, the shipment is delivered direct to us without loss of time and at a minimum of shipping expense. We receive it at our Service Building, a million dollar structure advantageously located in the heart of the Bush Terminal property.

Here the special facilities and equipment of the Service Building are brought into play and the shipment is unloaded and, according to instructions, is repacked and reshipped to the various points of destination, or any part of it can be warehoused for future shipment. In charge of this repacking are experts who have an intimate knowledge of the shipping requirements of all foreign countries.

The Umbrella and Cane showroom is attractive in its appointments

The South American shipment referred to may be consigned to a point that involves mule-pack delivery across the Andes or small-boat transportation up the Amazon.

The shipment for Russia demands special packing to meet the handling and exposure to which it will be subjected before reaching destination. The requirements of these forwarding problems are accurately known and carefully met by the experts in charge.

Spacious rooms are provided where an adequate
dining room exhibit may be shown

The shipment to the Southern or to the New England point is despatched by the safest, quickest, most economical route, depending on conditions, destination, etc., and all details incident to the transaction receive careful attention.

In cases of foreign shipments, customs, clearance insurance, and other necessary matters, are looked after by men of special training, and all instructions are given

Effective Shoe display may be secured by showcases of special design

in the languages read by the various handlers of the goods en route.

The experience and facilities necessary for the perfect handling of all these out-of-the-ordinary shipping and packing details are not always available in the plant of the average American manufacturer. But, even when they are present, to have the responsibilities lifted entirely from the shipper is a point of business economics and despatch worthy of more than passing notice.

The never-ending varieties of Toys will find ample room for display

Bird's-eye view of Bush Terminal

View of new Bush Terminal Service Building

Bush Terminal

The diversified service of Bush Terminal offers the logical solution to the problem of having an Eastern factory or assembling plant, a stock room or forwarding point—the national gateway not only to foreign countries but to the market of 20,000,000 people living within 200 miles of New York.

The plant covers 200 acres. There are 123 warehouses, sixteen industrial buildings, and the most modern cold storage installation in New York.

We have thirty miles of railroad tracks and own our own locomotives, automobile trucks, floats, lighters and tow boats. Jutting from the plant are eight of the largest piers in New York, where steamers to all parts of the world load and discharge their cargoes. It is the recognized terminal of every American railroad or its Atlantic Seaboard connections.

The entire plant is equipped with a sprinkler system—installed at a cost of $1,000,000—which enables tenants to receive the lowest rates in either mutual or stock insurance companies.

Users of the plant as an Eastern or Export Terminal have only to ship their goods, by any railroad, to Bush Terminal, New York. We receive the shipment, put it in warehouse, and, when instructed, separate it into lots as ordered, mark and re-ship, all for a few cents for each hundred pounds. On merchandise arriving or departing by any railroad, and by many steamship lines, there is no cartage charge. Where local deliveries to customers are required, we make a moderate cartage and lighterage charge.

We can attend to your Custom House Work and make collections for you, if necessary.

Those who avail themselves of our Warehousing Service can here carry a stock of goods in New York for immediate delivery to any point in Eastern or Export markets, at a trifling cost.

Those who desire to establish a plant or factory branch in New York will find in our Industrial Buildings every convenience, facility and cost-reducing factor co-ordinated in a way not found in any other locality. Space can be procured in any desired amount and added to as your requirements grow. Tenants are free from the usual burdens and limitations of the average New York headquarters.

For a more complete explanation of the economic advantages of Bush Terminal, with special reference to your own business or needs, write for particulars.

APR 19 1919

Executive Offices, 100 Broad Street, New York

Printed by Libri Plureos GmbH in Hamburg,
Germany